GW01368889

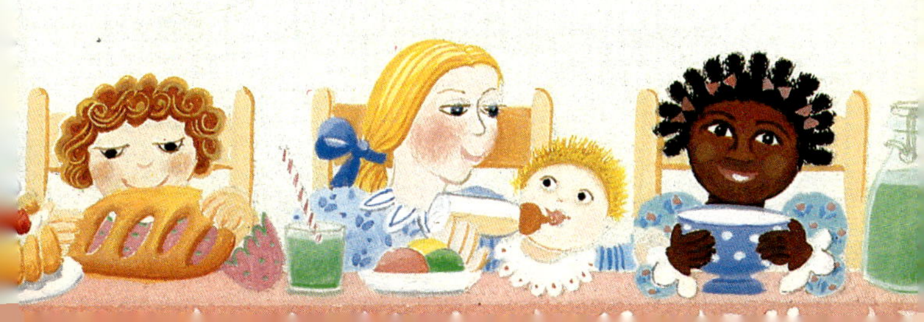

Written by Catherine de Sairigné
Illustrated by Danièle Bour

Specialist adviser:
The National Dairy Council

ISBN 1 85103 028 X
First published 1987 in the United Kingdom by
Moonlight Publishing Ltd,
131 Kensington Church Street, London W8

© 1985 by Editions Gallimard
Translated by Sarah Matthews
English text © 1987 by Moonlight Publishing Ltd
Printed in Italy by La Editoriale Libraria

POCKET • WORLDS

Milk

Do you have milk for breakfast?

THE WORLD OF FOOD

Perhaps you have it on your cereal, or in a glass to drink.
Milk is used to make butter, cream, cheese, yogurt...

Where does milk come from?

It comes from animals which are called mammals, because the females have mammary glands which produce milk. It is the first food their babies have. In this magical garden, you can see all sorts of mammals. Do you know what they're called? You can see a woman in the garden, because people are mammals too, and mothers feed their babies with milk when they are newly born.

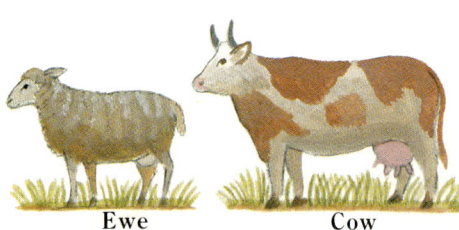

Female zebu

Nanny goat

Ewe

Cow

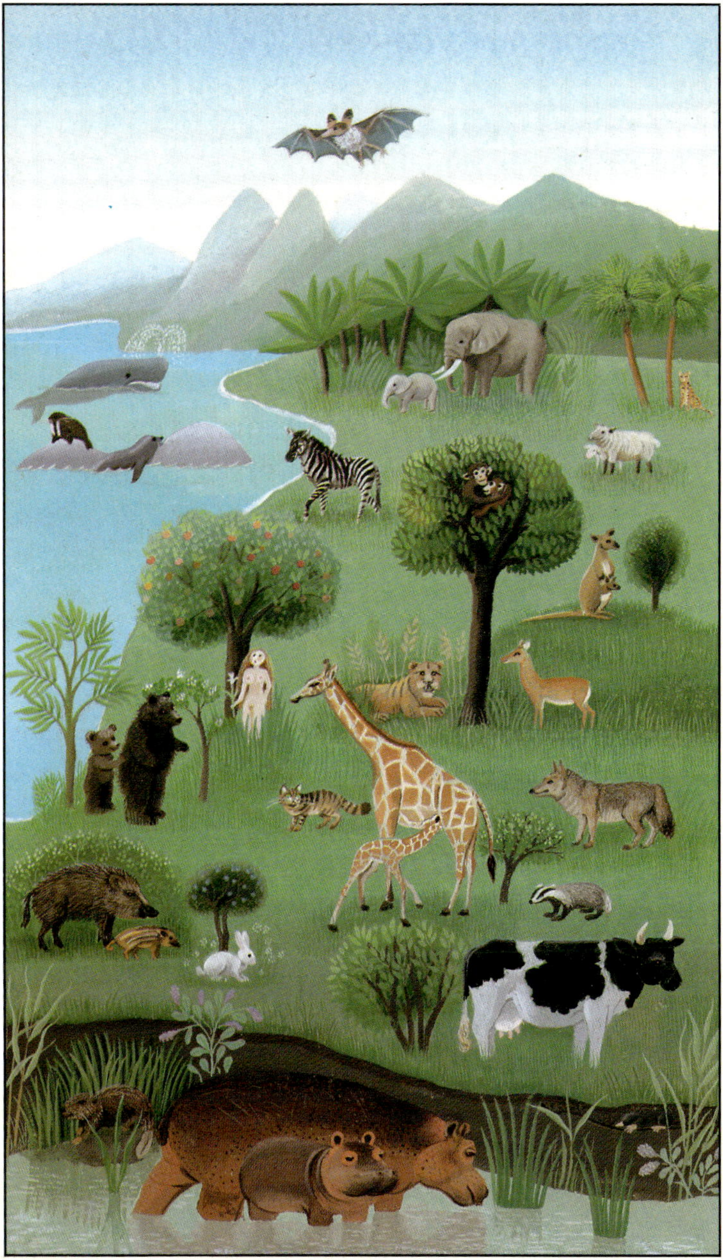

In Asia, Tibetans drink yaks' milk.

Do people drink only cows' milk?

No. People drink goats' milk, sheep's milk and, in some countries, asses' milk.

Mare

In parts of Africa and Asia people milk their herds of buffaloes, zebu and camels. The Lapps in Finland, Sweden and Norway milk the reindeer in the great herds which they follow.
As the reindeer are half wild, this can sometimes be a bit tricky!

The Indians in the Andes drink llamas' milk.

Do all milks taste the same?

Some taste stronger than others, some taste sour, others are sweet and delicious. Reindeer milk is very fatty; it is four times as fatty as cows' milk. This helps the baby reindeer keep out the cold better.

Indian buffaloes

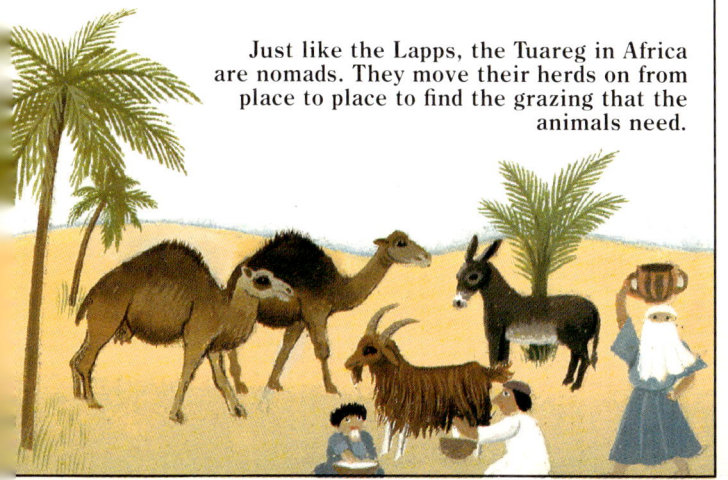

Just like the Lapps, the Tuareg in Africa are nomads. They move their herds on from place to place to find the grazing that the animals need.

Milk is a wonderful food: **it contains everything that baby animals need to grow up big and strong.**
A lamb drinks only its mother's milk, and yet in two months it doubles its birth weight. A baby whale grows a hundred kilos a day!

And you too fed on hardly anything except milk for the first six months of your life. You should go on drinking it for as long as you are growing.

Why is milk good for you?

It has calcium to strengthen your bones and teeth, proteins which help build up your muscles and body tissue, and fat and lactose (the sugar that is in milk) to keep you warm and give you energy.

There is a lot of water in milk as well, and a lot of vitamins. Meat and eggs, with their proteins, vegetables and fresh fruit, with their vitamins and fibres, are all very good for you too. You should eat and drink a little of all these kinds of food every day.

These are all foods which will help you grow strong and healthy – especially topped up with a glass of milk!

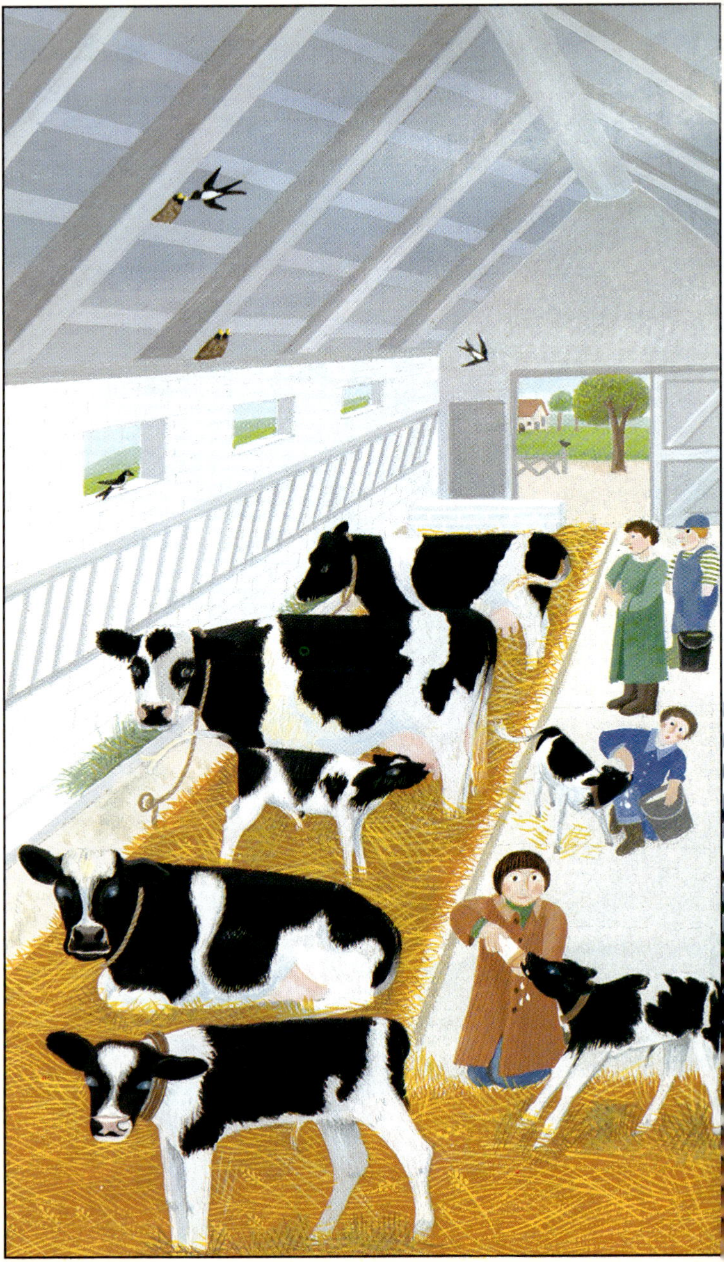

When does a cow give milk?

When she has a calf. As soon as the calf is born, the cow's udders fill with milk to feed it. She continues to give milk for ten months, around twenty litres a day.

A cow has a calf every year.

By the time she is six or seven, she is growing old and gives less milk. A cow will have four or five calves in her life, and will give over 30,000 litres of milk: enough to fill two big tankers!

As the calf grows up, the cow has milk to spare for the farmer.

What does a dairy cow eat?

Because he wants her to give lots of good milk, the farmer makes sure that his cow eats well. In winter, she stays in a cowshed, and eats hay, corn, barley, beets, soya... In summer, she grazes in the fields. Every day, she drinks at least six buckets full of water and eats ninety-five kilos of food. Just before the calf is born, the farmer gives the cow even more to eat.

Cows are ruminants. They need to chew grass again and again in order to digest it.

Today, scientists study very carefully the kind of food which cows eat, to be sure that the cows give as much of the best kind of milk as possible.

15

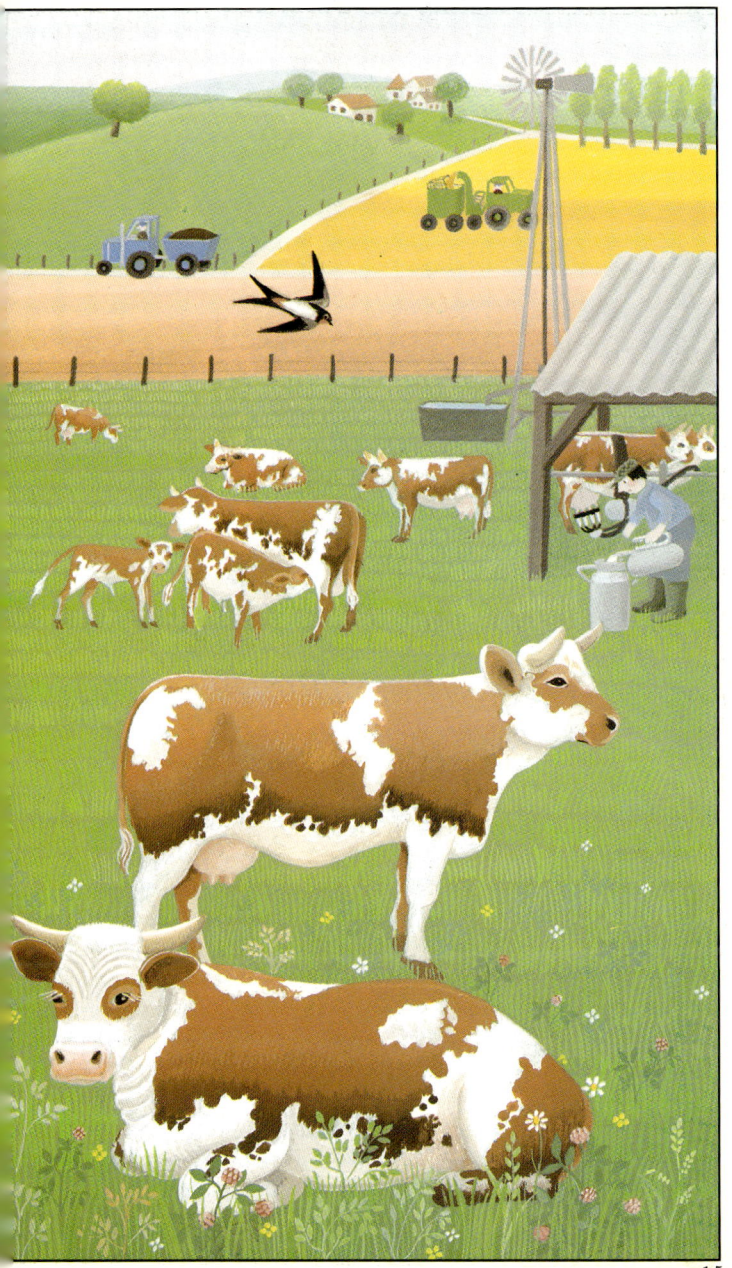

How do you milk a cow by hand?

This is the old-fashioned way of milking a cow; hardly anybody does it by hand any more. You have to squeeze the teat downwards very gently but firmly so as to squeeze out the milk, in the same way that the calf does when it sucks its mother's teat. There are lots of different cows. Some are popular in Great Britain (1, 2, 3), some are more usual on the Continent (4, 5, 6).

1. Friesian

2. Jersey

3. Ayrshire

Cows must be relaxed when they are being milked. Some farmers play music to them. This makes them calm and happy, and they give more milk.

4. Montbeliarde   5. Normandy   6. Salers

17

18

In the olden days, people used to drink milk just as it came out of the udder. But, untreated like this, milk does not stay fresh for long; very soon tiny germs, called **bacteria**, begin to grow. Some of them can cause diseases.

Bacteria seen much larger than life, under a microscope

What Louis Pasteur discovered

Louis Pasteur was a French scientist in the 19th century. He found that it was possible to kill these bacteria by heating the milk to a very high temperature for a few seconds. Milk that had been 'pasteurised' in this way could be kept safely for several days.

Pasteur's discovery meant that at last townspeople could enjoy fresh milk regularly.

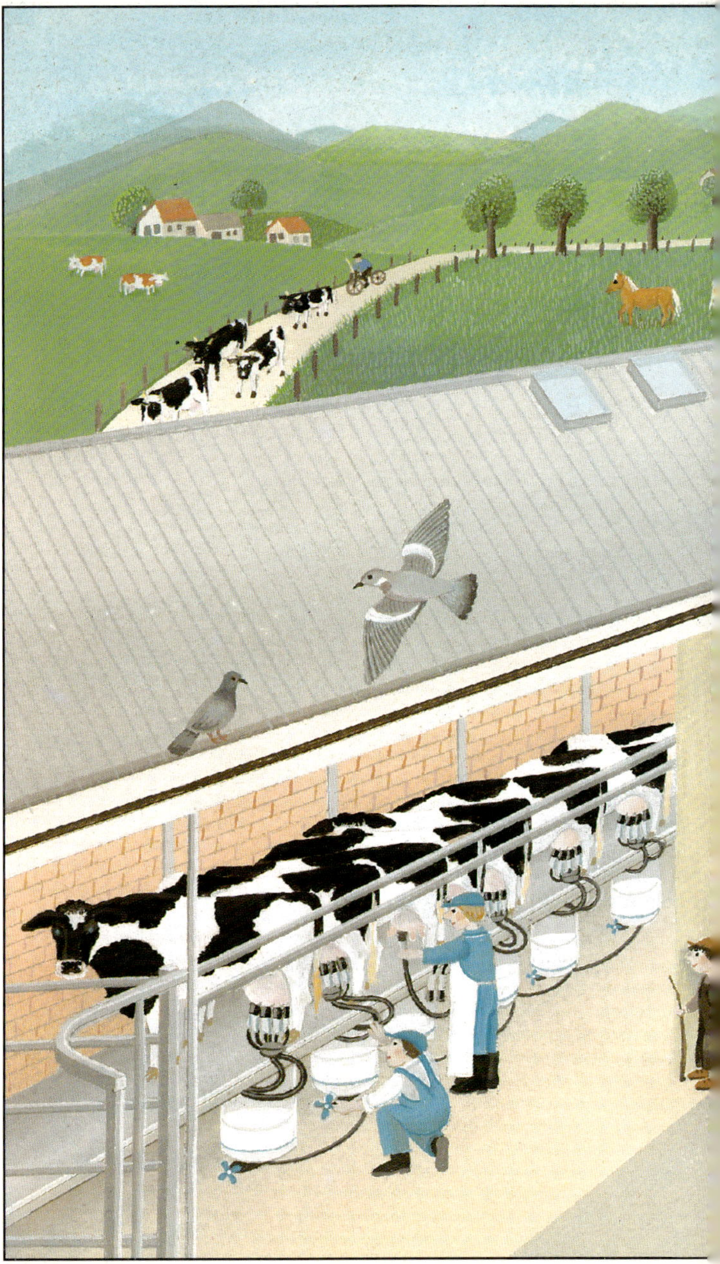

Nowadays, farmers use milking machines to help them milk their cows.

While milking them, the farmer gives his cows something to eat. This keeps them calm and makes them easier to milk. Their udders are wiped clean. A milking machine sucks out the milk to the tank, where it is cooled down to a temperature of 4°C. An insulated milk-tanker calls every day to collect the milk from the farm.

At the dairy, the milk can be treated in various ways. Sometimes the cream is taken off, to make skimmed milk. Sometimes milk is treated to break up the cream and make homogenised milk. But all the milk which goes through the dairy is heated up to at least 72°C for 15 seconds and then cooled very quickly to about 4°C. After that the pasteurised milk is put into bottles or cartons. The cartons are stamped with a use-by date.

A chilly chain

From the moment the cow has been milked the milk is kept in refrigerated tanks. It travels to the dairy or the shop in insulated tankers which keep it cool.

In most parts of Britain, the milkman delivers your milk to the doorstep every day, whatever the weather.

24

This is an old-fashioned dairy where they are making cream and butter.

Fresh cream and whipped cream

A separator (1) spins round very fast and separates the cream from the milk. The cream is a thick liquid full of fat. It is used to make butter: the cream is tipped into a churn (2), where it is beaten hard. It turns yellow and becomes firm. A liquid runs off: buttermilk. The bits of fat that were in the cream have stuck together. When they have been washed and shaped, either in a mould (3) or between pats, the butter is ready. If butter is salted, it keeps longer.

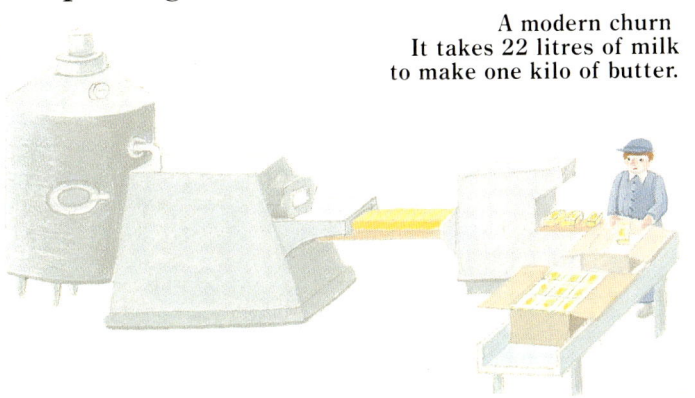

A modern churn
It takes 22 litres of milk to make one kilo of butter.

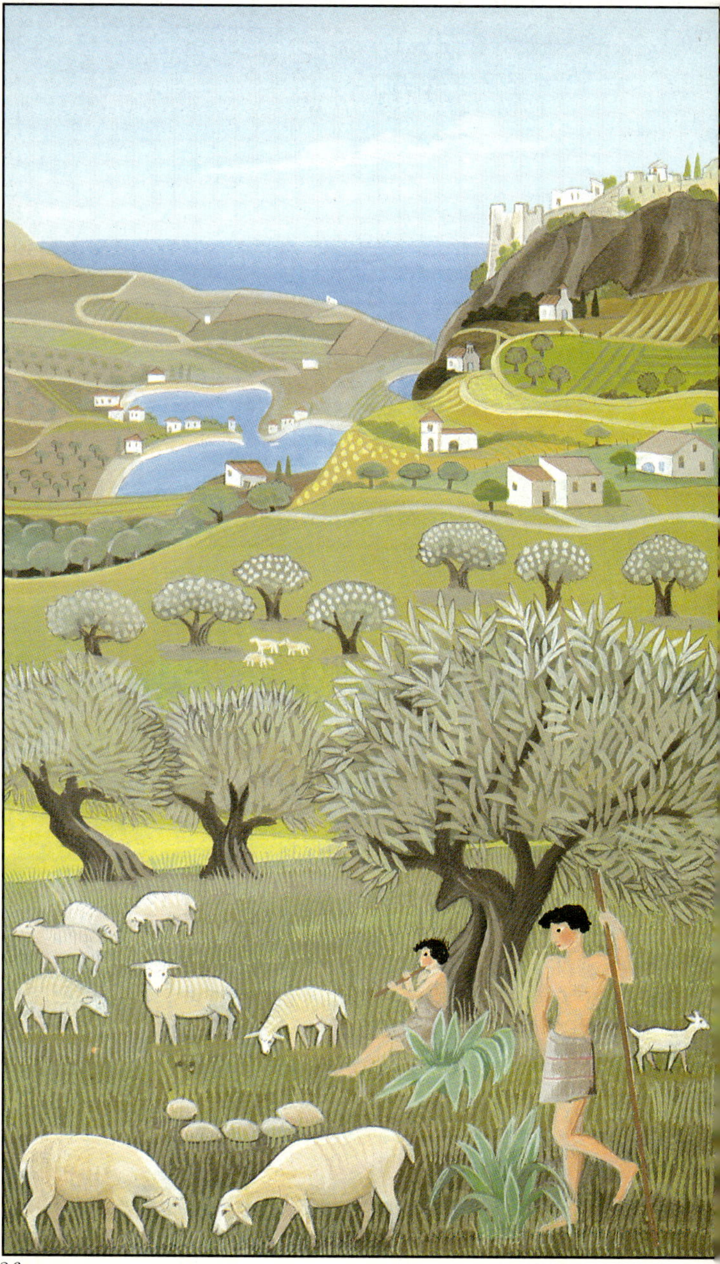

Cheese moulds, called drainers

When did people start milking cows?

Over 5,000 years ago. Then they learned to make cheese to use up the milk which they couldn't keep fresh. Cheese is made from the milk of cows, sheep and goats. Every region in the world makes its own sort of cheese. There are cream cheeses, or cheeses with hard rinds like Cheddar. In blue cheeses like Stilton and Gorgonzola, the tiny blue veins are produced by a minute fungus. Reindeer cheese is as hard as rock. Lapps often dunk it in their coffee before eating it.

Cream cheese

Traditional cheese-making

Different cheeses are made in different ways, but they all start off with **curdling.** The milk is warmed, and then 'starter' is added, to make the milk go sour. Next **rennet**, from a calf's stomach, is put in. This makes the milk clot and set. The milk has turned into **curds** and **whey.** After this, the liquid whey is drained off, either from a tap or through a bag.

Hard cheeses
have to be **pressed.**
Some, like Cheddar, are mixed
with salt and then pressed.
Others, like Gruyère,
are rubbed with salt
afterwards. 
When the cheese is
made, it is
left in store
to **mature.**
Cheddar is usually
kept for 5 months, but Mature Cheddar
is kept for at least 10 months.

There are thousands of different kinds of cheese in the world. In England there are nine traditional hard cheeses, such as Cheddar, Double Gloucester, and Wensleydale.

Goat's cheese, France

Crottin de chèvre, France

Camembert, France

Roquefort, France

Cantal, France

Quark, Germany

Edam, Holland

Emmenthal, Switzerland

Gorgonzola, Italy

Stilton, England

Double Gloucester, England

Parmesan, Italy

Manchego, Spain

Feta, Greece

Chanakh, USSR

Tilsit, Germany

Cheddar, Canada

White cheese, Mexico

Cream cheese, USA

Brick, USA

Beda, Egypt

Kosher cheese, Israel

Domestic cheese, Japan

How many different kinds of milk are there?

Fresh pasteurised milk is the one you usually buy at the shops or from the milkman. It can be kept for four or five days in the fridge.

These are some of the different kinds of pasteurised milk you can buy.

Full-cream milk means that none of the cream has been taken out.

Semi-skimmed means that nearly half the cream has been taken out and **skimmed** means that it has no cream at all.

Channel Islands milk is particularly rich in cream.

Sterilised milk is heated to 112°C for 15 to 40 minutes.

UHT milk (UHT means ultra-heat-treated) is flash-heated to a very high temperature, 132°C, for just over one second. If the carton is not opened, UHT milk keeps for at least three months.

Condensed milk is milk from which most of the water has been evaporated. You can get it in tins, either sweetened, with sugar added, or unsweetened. It will keep in the unopened tin for a year or more.

Powdered milk, also called dried milk, will keep for a year or more in an unopened carton, and for two or three weeks even after it has been opened. It takes eleven litres of milk to make one kilo of powdered milk.

Yogurt is milk which has been warmed and fermented. This thickens it and gives it a special sharp taste.

Here are two recipes for you to try.
Super striped delight:
Take as many different coloured jellies as you can. Ask a grown-up to dissolve each one in a separate bowl. Add a carton of yogurt to each bowl – either plain yogurt, or a fruit yogurt to match the jelly. Mix well. Pour one colour into

a clear dish and set in the fridge for
15 minutes. Then add the rest in stripes.

Banana bonanza:
In a mixing-bowl, mash a banana
with a fork. Add a teaspoonful of sugar
and quarter of a litre of milk (half a
pint). Beat the mixture well with your
fork or with a beater and at the last
minute add the juice of half a lemon.
Pour the mixture into a glass and serve
it to your favourite person (or drink it
yourself!).

Index

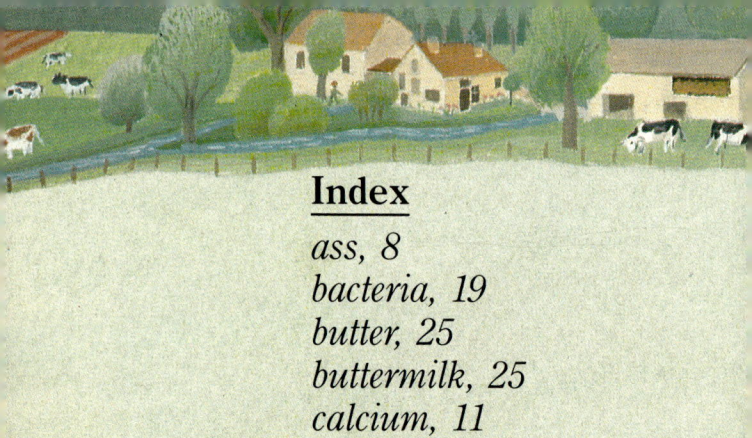

ass, 8
bacteria, 19
butter, 25
buttermilk, 25
calcium, 11
calf, 13
Cheddar, 28-29, 31
cheese, 11, 27
cheese-making, 28-29
cheese moulds, 27
churn, 25
condensed milk, 33
corn, 14
cow, 6, 13-14, 16
cream, 25
cream cheese, 27, 31
curdling, 28
curds, 27-28
dairy, 22, 25
draining, 28

fat, 11
food content, 10-11
food for cows, 14
Gorgonzola, 27, 31
mammals, 6
maturing, 29
milking, 13, 16, 20, 22
milkman, 23
Pasteur, Louis, 19
pasteurised, 19, 23, 32
pressing, 29
protein, 11
recipes, 34-35
refrigeration, 23
reindeer cheese, 27
rennet, 28
separator, 25
tankers, 23
tanks, 23
udders, 19, 22
vitamins, 11
whey, 28
yogurt, 34

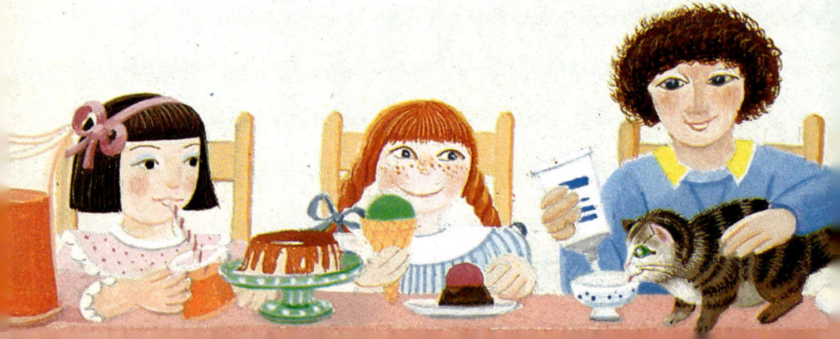